GIRAFFES
JIRAFAS

AMY CULLIFORD
Traducción de Pablo de la Vega

A Crabtree Roots Book
Un libro de Las Raíces de Crabtree

T0020274

Crabtree Publishing
crabtreebooks.com

School-to-Home Support for Caregivers and Teachers

This book helps children grow by letting them practice reading. Here are a few guiding questions to help the reader with building his or her comprehension skills. Possible answers appear here in red.

Before Reading:

• What do I think this book is about?
  - *I think this book is about giraffes.*
  - *I think this book is about what giraffes like to do.*

• What do I want to learn about this topic?
  - *I want to learn what giraffes drink.*
  - *I want to learn what colors a giraffe can be.*

During Reading:

• I wonder why...
  - *I wonder why giraffes are tall.*
  - *I wonder why giraffes eat so much.*

• What have I learned so far?
  - *I have learned that giraffes can run.*
  - *I have learned that giraffes drink water.*

After Reading:

• What details did I learn about this topic?
  - *I have learned that giraffes have long necks.*
  - *I have learned that giraffes can be white, yellow, and brown.*

• Read the book again and look for the vocabulary words.
  - *I see the word **tall** on page 6 and the word **drink** on page 12. The other vocabulary word is found on page 14.*

This is a **giraffe**.

Esta es una **jirafa**.

Most giraffes are white, yellow, and brown.

La mayoría de las jirafas son blancas, amarillas y cafés.

Most giraffes are **tall**.

La mayoría de las jirafas son **altas**.

All giraffes can run.

Las jirafas pueden correr.

Most giraffes eat all day.

La mayoría de las jirafas comen todo el día.

All giraffes **drink** water.

Todas las jirafas **beben** agua.

Words to Know
Palabras para conocer

drink
beben

giraffe
jirafa

tall
altas

28 Words

This is a **giraffe**.

Most giraffes are white, yellow, and brown.

Most giraffes are **tall**.

All giraffes can run.

Most giraffes eat all day.

All giraffes **drink** water.

39 palabras

Esta es una **jirafa**.

La mayoría de las jirafas son blancas, amarillas y cafés.

La mayoría de las jirafas son **altas**.

Las jirafas pueden correr.

La mayoría de las jirafas comen todo el día.

Todas las jirafas **beben** agua.

ZOO ANIMAL FRIENDS
ANIMALES AMISTOSOS DEL ZOOLÓGICO

GIRAFFES
JIRAFAS

Written by: Amy Culliford

Designed by: Rhea Wallace

Series Development : James Earley

Proofreader: Janine Deschenes

Educational Consultant: Marie Lemke M.Ed.

Photographs:
Shutterstock: Gastan Piccinetti: cover; Chaithanya Krishan:
p. 1; Bambi2020: p. 3, 14; RMFerreira: p. 5; Smithy55: p. 7, 14;
Jeannette Katzier: p. 8; JOel Shawn: p. 11; Stacey Ann Alberts:
p. 12-13, 14

Crabtree Publishing

Printed in Printed in China/082022/FE052422CT

Published in
Canada
Crabtree Publishing
616 Welland Ave.
St. Catharines, Ontario
L2M 5V6

Published in the
United States
Crabtree Publishing
347 Fifth Avenue,
Suite 1402-145
New York, NY, 10016

Library and Archives Canada Cataloguing
    in Publication
Available at the Library and Archives Canada

Library of Congress Cataloging-in-
    Publication Data
Available at the Library of Congress

Paperback: 9781039803015
Ebook: 9781039803138
Epub: 9781039803077